THE END OF IMMIGRATION

The Handbook to End All Immigration,

Illegal & Legal

By

M A Farrell

This book is from the series:

Fire the Federal Government

FIRST EDITION

Printed on acid-free paper

Library of Congress Cataloging-in-Publication Data has been applied for.

ISBN: 9781519384010

Author's note:

Recent attacks on Paris

Real events sometimes coincide with written speculation. This book was finished one week prior to the unconscionable attacks perpetrated against the people of Paris and, hence, France.

I decided to leave the opening few paragraphs as originally penned, even though they hint of pouring salt into an open wound.   This is not my intent. This book's ink was dry before the attacks took place. It is unfortunate that a great epiphany was not required to predict these sad events. It does, however strengthen the claim that, for the West, time is running out.

It is tragic that France, along with all of Europe, have thrown open their borders to immigrant populations, dangerous immigrants. I can only hope that this vicious assault upon the French people will cause all Western societies to reassess their immigration policies.

To that end, perhaps some of the ideas contained within this book may prove helpful.

Vive La France!

The Syrian example

The latest wave of Middle East immigration, self-imposed by the West, is another attempt to rescue the inevitable dross of failed nations. It may appear on the surface as a humanitarian gesture, rescuing poor souls from oppressive situations that are life-threatening. However, it continues to sow the seeds of Western Civilization's destruction and will eventually import jihadism into our midst. It is incredibly dangerous.

As millennial feuds between unenlightened, regressive nations reignite over and over and develop into open warfare, will the West continue to impose inapplicable values and failed policies to create even more international chaos? Probably. And this will result in even greater human tragedy than we are viewing today in Syria.

Will we, the West, respond to this and all future tragedies in the same manner, swamping our nations with refugees? Inviting into our lands thousands, eventually totaling millions of people that share none of the values that have, over centuries, stitched our cultural fabric together?

If so, Western culture is lost.

Political refugees are a small portion of the immigration problem that America and Europe are refusing to confront. The West is at a tipping point. England's open immigration policy towards its former colonies, self-flagellation for their colonial past, has already cast the British spirit to the wind. Vast immigration into France, Spain and Italy is relegating their cultures to history's dustbin. Germany is nearing a civil war over immigrants.

And the United States has begun the slide.

With the world's continued, unchecked population growth, the West is facing its greatest battle. Immigrants, legal or illegal, cannot be absorbed in increasing numbers, lest we abandon all hope of maintaining our culture along with any hope for an enlightened world.

Democracy is not gaining ground. Throughout the world one totalitarian regime is falling to another even more oppressive. America is the last, great lamp illuminating the preeminence of individual over state. However, we can only serve this mission as an example, not a haven. To do otherwise will surely extinguish that light.

Running out of time

The world is at a turning point that will determine the fate of our nation. We will go one of two directions. The *path-of-less* encompasses famine, poverty, ignorance, drudgery, disease, premature death and totalitarianism. The *path-of-more* is contrary. It is about creating abundance, wealth, enlightenment, self-fulfillment, health, decades of life extension and expanded freedom for the individual.

Almost daily we hear of advancements across the broad spectrum of science: decoding our DNA, gene therapies, building microscopic machines via nanotechnology, growing replacement human organs, understanding and exploring our universe and developing new sources of energy. All are marvels made possible through our high standard of living and the surplus wealth it generates. And all of it eventually permeates the world.

Since this nation's beginning, our gift to the world has been our ideals, our discoveries and our creations. *We are the light of the world. A city that is set on a hill that cannot be hidden.*

But our standard of living is in peril. Our surplus has evaporated and along with it a brilliant future for mankind. Our middle class, who is responsible for the bulk of our tax base, is shrinking. Our social programs, our schools, our hospitals, our parks, our emergency rooms and our jails are swamped with illegal immigrants. We can no longer afford to provide these services to our own citizens because illegals are draining the programs.

The hard decision

We can have a future that, if viewed today, would fill us with awe and wonder. It is obvious to rational individuals that the *path-of-more* is the most desirable. But this requires a determination and resolution never before mustered by our nation. There is a tough decision for all of us to confront. If we choose the *path-of-more,* we will find it a hard path, a very hard path indeed. For the *path-of-more* comes with a caveat.

It is not available to all that currently live upon this planet. Some people will experience a bright future while others are left to scrabble.

This is an objectionable idea to a nation steeped within the ideals of equality among peoples, sanctity of human life and, for liberals, being our brother's keeper. The alternative is that we all are left to scrabble. And the lights of that *shining city on the hill* are extinguished forever.

Why cannot we eventually expand the *path-of-more* to all peoples? If the United States can achieve this future, why cannot it be extended to other countries? It is said capitalism *raises all boats*. Why not in this circumstance?

Because of *time*. America is out of time. The world is out of time.

The problem

There are too many people on this planet. And all want access to *our* standard of living.

They want in.

If we allow this, our own standard of living will plummet. There are too many people for the boats at hand. They would never rise under the weight. Hence the *path-of-less*: famine, ignorance, drudgery, disease, premature death and totalitarianism.

In 1950, the world had approximately 2.1 billion people. Today it has over 7 billion. It is estimated that by 2050 there will be between 9.5 and **12 billion** (depending upon wars, disease and starvation). Earth has less than 200 million square miles of surface area. When you subtract oceans, deserts, high mountains and land considered uninhabitable, this leaves about 20% livable land for humans (a generous estimate). That calculates to 40 million square miles. Divided among 7 billion people, this translates to .0057 square miles per person or 158 thousand square feet or 3.65 acres.

That may sound adequate. However, from this we must deduct roads, parking lots, housing developments, condos, apartment buildings, commercial buildings, industrial buildings, military bases, government buildings, city parks, state parks, national parks, camp grounds, airports, railroads and every other physical component of what we refer to as civilization. Additionally, we would have to grow our own crops and raise poultry and animals on our own portion of land as there would be nothing left for agriculture.

Imagine what the world will be like with 9.5 **billion** people.

Then imagine after 2050. The world's population will continue to expand. Unless massive famine, disease or the conflagration of world war intercedes. If so, we will experience the dystopian future so prevalent in today's books and movies.

Population growth *rates* have slowed in some of the most populous nations: China, India, and Latin America. However, slowing an exponential growth *rate* is not close to slowing overall population growth.

If we are out of time to reverse the world's population growth, what shall we do?

We could always build our buildings taller to house more people in a smaller space. Perhaps we could live underwater in the oceans. With the polar icecaps melting, we could build upon the sparse, rocky ground left behind. Outer space is always an option.

Or we can accept that dystopian future.

The question becomes: why should we have to live this way? Why should we merely *exist*, as do so many around the globe?

Consider this. We have already extended the lives of people within poorer countries through clean water, vaccinations, antibiotics, plant yields and foreign aid (in the form of food stocks). We have dramatically lowered the mortality rate of their infants. And what comes from this generosity? Increased populations demanding a piece of us.

Somehow the elitists that wield influence within our country have convinced the rest of us that we are responsible for everything bad that happens in the world and that we are constantly in need of atonement: giving away resources and wealth; allowing invasion of more and more indigent masses from failed nations.

We must reject this thinking. On multiple occasions, we have defeated evil forces in defense of the world's freedom, sacrificing our precious blood and treasure. We have rebuilt nations of our allies and former enemies and still shield them. And regardless of what the elitists command academes to preach to our children, we do not support our lifestyle through the exploitation of innocent peoples abroad.

We are constantly rushing aid to victims of international disasters. Yet America can match the desolate stories of misfortune that incessantly bombard us from undeveloped nations. We have our own natural disasters: floods, hurricanes, tornados, earthquakes, droughts, wildfires, disease outbreaks.

These have occurred since we first set foot upon this continent. Yet no other country ever came to our aid. We have survived our own disasters. We spend **billions** of dollars every year to help other countries contend with such problems. And what do we receive for our generosities? Scorn and ridicule. If we act, liberals say we are Imperialists. If we sit idle, they say we are selfish and shortsighted.

Our moral skirts are clean. We have done enough for the world and now it is time we save ourselves. There is a gathering storm. It will not be a conventional confrontation of the past where armor and infantry are poised at borders. It will occur as the new model of invasion: immigration. The *have* nations are the target. And the *have-not* nations (aka, *failed* nations) are producing more weapons daily. These weapons of mass destruction are called *people*.

We must steel ourselves for the hard path ahead. And we must select the leaders that have the fortitude to lead us down that path.

Immigration was never our Founders' policy

It is politically savvy to spout, "We are a nation of immigrants." However, this is not how our nation began.

Of the 56 signers of the Declaration of Independence, there were only 6 that were not born in the newly declared United States. They were: George Taylor,

James Wilson, Matthew Thornton, Francis Lewis, John Witherspoon and Button Gwinnett. All six led accomplished lives and all six displayed admirable courage by signing the dangerous document. Yet none would be on the short list we refer to as our *Founding Fathers*. The men we acknowledge most often with that honorific are: John Adams, Thomas Jefferson, Benjamin Franklin, Samuel Adams, and John Hancock. (George Washington was in Boston, forging an army. James Madison did not publicly take the stage until the Constitutional Convention, eleven years later. Yet both of these men should be considered as upon the list).

These Founding Fathers were not immigrants. Many of these men could trace their ancestry back generations to the founding of the New World Colonies. They were not creating a new nation for immigrants. As they were all derived of former European stock, they were establishing a new Europe within a new order; English law, Greek and Roman political structures, all infused with Enlightenment philosophy. Nothing indicates they were opposed to immigration, if it were European. However it was not a paramount issue for the Continental Congress.

The Statue of What?

Little more than a hundred years after these men penned their lofty goal, the United States was presented a representational gift of brotherhood from France. It was The Statue of Liberty, designed by

Frenchman Frédéric Auguste Bartholdi. The statue's actual title is *Liberty Enlightening the World*. It was Bartholdi's intent that *Liberta*, the Roman goddess of liberty, represent America's light-to-the-world, illuminating freedom, liberty and self-determination.

It was not created as a welcome mat for immigrants.

The French made the statue, but left it to us to provide the land along with the cost of creating a pedestal. The U.S. government provided an island within New York. But private funds were sought to build the base. One fund-raising event occurred wherein an accomplished poet and political writer, Emma Lazarus, donated a poem at auction. It was entitled *The New Colossus*.

Lazarus, born of Sephardic Jewish parents, worked tirelessly to aid Jewish immigrants arriving in America. Many were survivors of Eastern Europe's pogroms. Lazarus' ode strummed emotional sentiments. *Tired, poor, huddled masses, homeless, tempest-tost* expressed her sympathies towards her ethnic people while giving written scenery to their plight. It was an effective voice lifted against a moral wrong.

Yet, if our Founding Fathers had known that future citizens, flooding into their magnificent experiment of nation-building, would be described with such adjectives, it is most certain they would have crinkled their noses, as if some foul odor had offended their senses. And in no manner did Lazarus' words express

American governmental policy. It did not even express majority opinion within America.

During Lazarus' time, the continuing flood of immigrants from Ireland was causing immense problems within New York City and Boston. Revulsion of immigrant slums, crime, poverty, illiteracy and disease was more prevalent than starry-eyed sentiments of welcoming more *huddled masses* to America's *teeming shores*.

Ms. Lazarus' poem was interpreted such that the Statue of Liberty held the lamp of welcome for arriving immigrants. It is true that the statue is one of the first recognizable landmarks eastern immigrants arriving on our shores viewed. And, after a long sea voyage in steerage, it must have been an emotional moment for those first spying *Liberta*. But that was not the reason for the existence of the statue.

Within her last line, Ms. Lazarus' poem has misled all succeeding generations when she spoke for *Liberta*:

I lift my lamp beside the golden door!

That lamp is lit as a beacon of liberty on which the world can model itself. It is not a porch light illuminating an open door, welcoming refugees from every failed state that refuses to heed our example.

For Ms. Lazarus, America was a way-station for fellow Jews, not a final destination. She dreamt of a Zionist state and championed this ideal throughout her life. She should be applauded for this effort. And she should not be blamed for merely offering a poem to be sold at auction to benefit the building of the statue's pedestal. The person deserving of rebuke is her friend, Georgina Schuyler, who campaigned for nearly two decades to have the words of *Colossus* immortalized upon a plaque within the pedestal.

Now, due to sentiment trumping reason once again, we are expected to fashion immigration policy upon poetic words as if they were a national charter, ordained by Congress. Mass immigration never had a federal charter. As this plaque reflected the opinion of a few over the, then, majority of Americans, the words should be dismounted and re-auctioned to the private sector. The funds are required elsewhere.

The ticking bomb

According to the United States Census Bureau (U.S.C.B.), our population was 281 million in year 2000. This same agency estimates our population will exceed 400 million by year 2050. That is an increase of nearly 142%. The fertility rate for all ethnic groups *except Hispanics* is less than 2.0. The number 2.0 refers to the number of children a woman has: two children would be an offset of one woman and one man. If the number is less than 2, then, theoretically, that ethnic group is decreasing (assuming that one male is not responsible for pregnancies of multiple females). That means population numbers of Whites, Asians, Native Americans and African Americans should drop. From where will the 142% increase derive?

Hispanics.

They have a fertility rate over 2.0 (2.35).

The U.S.C.B. states that 82% of projected population growth will occur from illegal immigrants and their offspring. The other 18% is from legal immigration.

The U.S. Department of Homeland Security, referencing a *Pew Research* report, estimates there are nearly **12 million** illegal immigrants in the United States as of 2012. The report states that within the 82% number, 77% are Hispanics (62% from Mexico with the balance 15% from other Central and South American countries).

The charge of racism

Any negative mention that singles out a minority group is quickly met with cries of *racism!* As regards immigration, this would indicate Americans were racist towards every ethnic group that ever immigrated to this country.

The charge is ludicrous.

If we were discussing this problem during the 1800's, percentages cited in the last section could apply to the Irish influx beginning in the mid 1800's. During the

1840's, a potato blight plunged the Emerald Isle into famine. Of the total Irish homeland population, one-third died from disease and starvation, one-third remained living within their country and one third emigrated. Of those emigrants, the vast majority had America as their destination. Between 1840 and 1905 over 3.5 million Irish came to America.

Technically, none within this immigration wave were illegal. With our Westward Expansion, the new America was an empty country. These Irish were allowed to legally enter, for a while, as they filled a need: cheap labor and cannon fodder.

A wild land needed taming, begun by clearing forests, then by milling the resulting wood into lumber. The building of railroads and canals needed strong backs and calloused hands. Textile mills required replacement women as latest generations of English and Scot workers refused this tedious work with its accompanying low pay.

And America's raging Civil War required new human grist to grind. Over 150,000 Irish immigrants were conscripted into the Union Army. And that same number again were recruited from the sons of previous generational Irish.

Although their physical labor and fighting ability were initially required by America, the Irish entered America burdened with an automatic handicap. A nation founded by Protestants (many being Scots-Irish) was threatened by this ever-increasing mass of devout Irish Catholics. The never-ending war between Ulster Protestants and Irish Catholics was imported to America. Riots broke out between Protestant Scots-Irish, who had been in America since its founding, and the newly arrived Irish-Catholics. It was not until 1960 that a Catholic had a chance of winning the highest elected office of the land, the Presidency. Although it was still a contentious issue throughout the campaign, this barrier was surmounted by the election of John Kennedy.

After four bloody years, the American Civil War finally concluded. Then, with the completion of the Trans-Continental railroad, the American West was finally joined to the East. The rush for free Western land ended shortly thereafter. Jobs for Irish became more difficult to find, especially with more and more immigrants arriving daily. Massive competition for the lowliest jobs created hardcore urban poverty which resulted in slums, tenements and soaring crime. Being Irish became a stigma. Their poverty, accompanied by heavily-accented English, and their lack of formal education gave them the collective portrayal as dunces and rubes. For Irish men, the hopelessness of grinding poverty was numbed through alcohol. For successful Protestants steeped in Calvinistic training of discipline, moderation and abstinence, Irish alcoholism only reinforced the view that the race was lazy, stupid and incapable of being educated.   A quote of the day demonstrates how far down the socio-economic scale sat the Irish. It said that Irish women domestics had "about the same intelligence as that of an old grey-headed Negro [sic]."

Job advertisements included the phrase "Irish need not apply." Lawn signs appeared notifying "Irish and dogs / Keep off the grass." Business establishments announced, "Irish enter through the back."

The Irish were not the only immigrants to suffer such treatment. In varying degrees it was applied to Italians, Poles, Jews, Indians, Asians and other ethnic groups coming to America. No matter the best intent of law, you cannot legislate feelings. However, racism was not the root cause. In the case of immigration, it derives from a self-defense mechanism, the defense of one's culture.

When an established people are told to make way for a significant percentage of new arrivals, resistance must be viewed as cultural defense, not some intrinsic malice or pathological need to inflict harm upon others. Resentment is a reaction not to be unexpected.

But resentment is not racism.

An important component of racism is exclusion of an ethnic group from not only mainstream society but from mainstream economic opportunities as well. This only occurred for one ethnic group: Black African Americans. Their destroyed social roots, through generations of forced bondage, coupled with a distinguishing skin color, made them victims of *real* racism. This remains an American problem. And we strive to correct the past and to make amends. But it does not apply to other ethnic groups.

When addressing the issue of illegal immigrants, charges of racism are leveled because an ethnic minority is involved. This is a subterfuge contrived by elitists and delivered through liberals. It is cited as racism to our children in public schools. Racism is the *red herring* used to shame Americans from resisting further invasion of our soil. Nothing within this article suggests or promotes any ill will towards legal citizens of our country regardless of ethnic background.

Assimilation is important

Large percentages of the same ethnic group entering over a short period of time creates less demand to assimilate into the larger, pre-existing culture. When one can immigrate to a new country yet live within a microcosm of his native country, where is the incentive to assimilate? When neighborhoods display store signs in one's native tongue; when clerks within that store speak one's native tongue; when media (radio, television, internet) is hosted, written and spoken by one's former countrymen; when one's neighborhood is filled with native speakers; and, significantly important, when the government of the new country co-prints official documents and signs in one's native tongue and teaches the children in the native tongue, what is the message being delivered?

One does not have to assimilate. And, yes, the above speaks to Hispanics. And that is factual, not racist.

Did not the Irish, Poles, Jews, Indians and Asians have their same enclaves, neighborhoods of native speakers and native language signs? Yes, however they were relatively small and, over time, lost their younger generations who learned English and moved away. Assimilation into American culture was a determined goal of parents. Hispanics, due to their native countries' proximity to the U.S., do not strive for assimilation with the same fervor. Their ever-growing numbers, are expanding their native spheres of influence. California, Texas, Arizona and New Mexico are becoming more Hispanic than American, in culture and tongue. Colorado and Nevada are at the beginning of the transformation as well.

It is poignant that a long-time phrase has fallen into disuse. Remember the term *The American melting pot*? That meant several different ethnic groups assimilate into one. But that does not mean all was accepted from each group.

To stay with the *melting pot* analogy, it begins with a cultural *broth*. This is the essence of American culture: why our country was founded. The broth includes such seasonings as: freedom, equality of opportunity, independence, law-abiding, patriotic, self-reliant, self-disciplined, educated, neighborly, spiritual, tolerant of others, free-enterprise, and reaping gain or loss from one's individual efforts. And the spoon that stirs all these ideals together is a single language, English.

Each new ethnic group that is added to the pot is like a new spice. It gives the broth character, a deeper, richer taste. But just as in any dish, if you dump in too much of one spice it overwhelms the taste of everything else. Any semblance to the old recipe is lost.

When too many of any one ethnic group swamp our nation, they cannot be properly blended into our pot. Instead, the broth is spoiled through transferred failures from third-world nations: government corruption, ceaseless poverty, lawlessness, depletion of natural resources, and illiteracy. And this leaves a foul taste for the rest of us.

Assimilation works the same as our melting pot analogy. A little at a time does not threaten the end result of the cultural pot. We can absorb and even be enriched by other cultures. Each ethnicity contributes its own identities and backgrounds, but the broth remains American. And just as a pot takes time to simmer, so assimilation takes time, usually two generations. We are speaking of nearly a hundred years. And, in lower numbers, assimilation is not threatening to the culture we have worked hard to establish.

In any nation, when assimilation is low or non-existent, there is another threat. It is called *Balkanization*.

To this point, America has been an incredibly successful experiment. At the moment of our national creation, there was one intrinsic ideal in which most of the world believed we would fail: the melting pot. They had good reason to be skeptical. Since man began assembling together in tribes to assure mutual protection, wars have been waged throughout the world over one tribe, or ethnicity, refusing to live alongside another. It still occurs today: Kurds, Basques, Tuaregs, Chechens, Rohingyans, Arabs and Jews, just to name a few.

In the past, a hotbed of ethnic clashes occurred constantly with the inhabitants of the Balkans (modern day Serbia, Croatia, Bosnia-Herzegovina, Bulgaria, Albania, Macedonia, Montenegro, Kosovo, Slovenia and Greece). And from these conflicts came the spark that ignited World War I. *Balkanization* has since become a term to describe unsettled power-sharing, borders and conflicts that constantly flare up anew. We are fortunate in this area. With so many different ethnic groups living together, America has been the world's example of tolerance within its own peoples. It is a monumental accomplishment. It defies all historical models and precedence.

Our success is due to assimilation and use of a common, native tongue. But how long will we maintain this success in the face of a whole-scale invasion?

It is not just lack of assimilation that has Americans resentful of, and angry at, illegal immigrants.

The Social Costs

As stated above, Hispanic illegal immigrants are arriving in such numbers that the rate of assimilation is low or non-existent. Many illegal Hispanics travel back and forth from America to their home country every year. They work here, earn money and send, or physically carry this money back home.

What is wrong with this? First, they are flouting our laws. If they are apprehended while crossing our border, they merely attempt a later crossing. There is no major penalty for trying. When one law is ignored, other laws are destined to be broken, which is born out in crime statistics (addressed further in this section). Also, according to the Bank of Mexico, over US$ 16 **billion** were sent to Mexico in family remittances last year. That adds to our trade deficit (though not included in official reporting). And, as illegals are often paid in cash, it is easily deduced that no U.S. taxes were collected upon these earnings.

A more serious problem involving immigrants is the financial pressure they place upon social services.

The U.S. spends **billions** of dollars annually to aid immigrants' assimilation via bilingualism. We provide governmental documents printed in multiple languages. By law, we provide court interpreters for any legal action against a non-English speaker. The Associated Press (AP) reported in 2003 that Virginia courts spent $2.7 **million** for this purpose. Take that cost and multiply it by all the court systems in our country. Now double that for the increase in immigration since 2003.

Most costly is bilingualism in our educational system. The federal *No Child Left Behind* Act forces bilingualism upon school districts or federal funds for education will be withheld. Another *AP* story of 2003 reported that New York City spent $20 **million** to support *one year* of bilingualism in its school system. These numbers are *tripling* every five years. The Department of Education reports that, for the 2012-2013 school year in six states (Alaska, California, Colorado, Nevada, New Mexico, and Texas), 10% or more of public school students were English language learners. This same group constituted **23%** of public school enrollment in California.

It is argued that bilingualism aids assimilation. It can be argued with equal veracity that it does the opposite. If one is able to navigate the educational system in the immigrant's native tongue, where is the incentive to assimilate? And if the immigrant is segregated along with others from his homeland, how does this encourage absorption of American culture?

Unlike some countries, we have designed our social services not to benefit all economic classes, only the needy. For instance, if we pay for health insurance, we receive no free medical service at a county hospital. Laws dictate that no hospital refuse care to a patient in the emergency room, regardless of citizenship or ability to pay. And any hospital will verify that emergency room care is the most expensive. Illegal immigrants, lacking medical insurance, flood our emergency rooms and use them as a clinic or doctor's visit. They bring children in for colds, cuts and bruises. The Obama Administration even uses this example as justification for creating tax-payer subsidized medical insurance. Yet this is only the administration's first step.   As illegal immigrants are a major percentage of emergency room patients, by their own goals the administration is obviously seeking to expand free health care insurance to all persons within our country, regardless of legal status. This would be the only way to impact soaring costs of emergency room care.

And the U.S. taxpayer will have to foot the bill for another endless-growth entitlement program that has no predetermined method of paying for itself. And a large chunk of taxes will be paying for non-American citizens that are here illegally.

The *Federation for American Immigration Reform* calculates that nearly $11 **billion** is credited to treatment of illegal aliens in emergency rooms. In the $2 **billion** of federal *Emergency Medicaid* annual funding, over half is estimated to pay for illegals. As these patients cannot be forced to provide proof of citizenship, it is difficult to prove their legal status. Nearly half of this funding goes to New York, Arizona, California and Texas; states with the largest illegal alien populations.

As to Welfare, illegal aliens are not legally eligible for benefits. However, as with most government programs there is a loophole. One of the ways illegal aliens use emergency rooms is to birth children at U.S. taxpayer expense. Our current law makes any child born on U.S. soil a U.S. citizen (a point covered later). These children have been referred to as *anchor babies* as their endowed citizenship provides an *anchor* for illegal mother and family to stay within our country. As the child is an American citizen, he or she is eligible for Welfare.

Staying with the medical theme, there is another area that is of great concern. Illegals are not vaccinated for many of the diseases we currently have under control or have eradicated within our country. In a report of the *Journal of American Physicians and Surgeons*, the group of doctors writing express deep concern with increases in multiple drug-resistant tuberculosis,

Chagas disease, dengue fever, polio, hepatitis A, B, and C; all brought into our country by illegal aliens. Some of these are diseases we have little history of (Chagas and dengue). Others have been kept under control (hepatitis). And some had been eradicated from within our borders (polio and tuberculosis). Now we must contend with this new threat to the public's health. Is this watching out for the welfare of our citizens?

Policing and incarceration are another societal cost. According to the *Center for Immigration Studies*, the *Department of Homeland Security* (DHS) estimates that 20% of all inmates in prison and jails are immigrants, legal and illegal. Some samplings of specific jail locations:

- o Maricopa County, Ariz.: **22%** of felons are **illegal** aliens;
- o Lake County, Ill.: **19%** of jail inmates are **illegal** aliens;
- o Collier County, Fla.: **20% to 22%** of jail inmates and arrestees are **illegal** aliens;
- o Weld County, Colo.: **12.8% to 15.2%** of those jailed are **illegal** aliens.

Whereas non-citizens comprise approximately 8.6% of the population, these high percentages are not necessarily an indictment of one ethnic group as much as pointing out a fact: massive immigration, legal or illegal, is a troubling source of crime. We already have concentrations of crime within our own citizen demographics. We need to focus our resources on this plight without importing crime from other nations.

Beyond the problem of public safety there is the issue of cost. According to a *CBS* News story, the U.S. has about 5% of the world population. Yet the story states we have nearly **25%** of the world's incarcerated persons. An organization, *The Price of Prisons*, states the average annual cost of incarceration is $31,307 per prisoner. In East Coast states this cost runs between $50,000 to $60,000 annually. This translates to **$63.4 billion** per year; a staggering sum that could be put to better use. And these statistics are from twelve years past.

This problem will not be solved overnight by halting immigration. It will, however, be substantially decreased. Why would we have any desire to increase this dilemma?

Effects of declining population

If every ethnic group, except Hispanics, has decreasing population numbers, then should we not use immigration to reverse this trend?

Absolutely not, for why would we want to reverse this trend? Was our country a lesser nation when we had a population of 125 Million? Or 250 Million? Today we look back at the times reflecting these lower numbers with a certain nostalgia, missing the self-reliant, law-abiding, respectful, freer and cohesive nation. A growing population is not something we should desire or steer public policy by. The opposite should be true.

But who will pick the crops? Who will blow our leaves?

Yes, some foods may cost more or even be in shortage for a few years. But this would be corrected by new technologies. Where an economic distortion occurs, free-enterprise will find a solution. Robotics is already developing mechanical hands with the sensitivity of a human's. They will be expensive at first and, hence, translate to higher prices. That will fall quickly once the market is open to automation. Cotton seeds had to be hand combed from bolls until Eli Whitney invented his cotton gin. Automated picking systems for citrus, cherries and apples already exist.

As to leaf blowing or lawn mowing, these too will be serviced by automation. We already have a robotic vacuum for inside of homes. It is not a stretch to see robotic lawnmowers and leaf collectors created. In the meantime, maybe our children can pitch in as they did for generations prior.

Beyond these minor concerns come the major benefits of a declining population. Would you not appreciate your child to be taught in a classroom size of 15 or even 10 rather than current trends of 30, 40 students or more? (Right now Washington State is essentially suing itself over mandates for classroom sizes less than

30 students. The current estimate to correct the situation would cost taxpayers **Billions** in new taxes. Billions is usually a term we associate with Federal spending, not State).

Here are additional benefits possible through a declining population.

What if our property taxes were lower because no new schools were needed? What if our commuter traffic were cut in half? How much gasoline would we save? How much more productive would our workforce be if it did not spend hours on the expressways? How much longer would our infrastructure last if it did not suffer the pounding and stress of maximum usage 24/7? How many police would we require if crime were cut in half? How much more attention could a doctor give us individually if he or she did not have to scurry from room to room to meet existing patient loads?

How much less would we have to pay in taxes to support social services if those services were not swamped by the lower economic class of which the vast majority of immigrants populate?

How much land could we take out of production for food stocks and, instead, have farmers reforest acreage instead of producing excess milk, wheat or corn?

How much would pollution of our air, water and soil decrease?

An issue few decline to discuss is our life-extension efforts. If, through genetics, we extend our lives to a hundred or more years, how would we support the combination of more persons living longer juxtaposed to more persons being born each year? With declining birthrates, this becomes a non-issue.

An intangible gift of a declining population is freedom. When a population continues to grow, freedom drops. More and more laws become necessary to define the individual's space and encroachments upon it. More laws equal more law-breakers. And this requires more policing. And more policing means greater restraints upon freedom.

There are so many benefits to a decreasing population that it is too lengthy to list here. But there are some that oppose such a decline in population.

Since the industrial revolution, corporations have enjoyed an ever-growing labor pool. This is beneficial to them as this allows excess population to compete for jobs. Translated, this means lower wages and higher unemployment. A growing population also expands revenues from increasing sales of goods and services. This results in higher corporate profits. Corporations do not want a shrinking labor pool or shrinking consumer numbers. They will oppose any steps to reduce our population, even in the face of falling employment opportunities.

Corporations have sent, and continue to send, American production line jobs overseas. And the few remaining in the U.S. are being automated via robotics. What will be the source of jobs for all of these immigrants, let alone our native citizenry? Why would we need an increased labor pool?

And this leads us to other groups that do not want to stop legal or illegal immigration.

Immigration Supporters

It should be of no surprise at the first group supporting unlimited immigration. It is the immigrants themselves. They wish to see more and more of their ethnicity move here. They send home tales of a land of milk and honey: high wage jobs (compared to where they came from); free medical care; free birthing hospitals; free food (if they have an *anchor baby* and receive welfare, or take advantage of numerous food banks); free education in their own tongue; free parks and beaches; free lawyers and interpreters if they are arrested; TV, radio and newspapers in their own tongue; no military service; clean water and air; abundance of sympathetic social agencies. And many, many relatives to help.

And, if they stay long enough, and enough of their relatives follow, eventually they can take to the streets in massive numbers, demanding legal citizenship. It has occurred before.

Through sheer numbers, illegals force the granting of legal status. Eventually they receive the right to vote. Then they demand immigration to be even easier. They certainly are not going to vote for candidates who oppose immigration. If President Obama (a Democrat) gave immunity and eventual citizenship to **12 million** illegal immigrants, which political party would they vote for; Republicans that speak against illegal immigration or Democrats that champion citizenship for this enormous block of new voters?

And this leads to the second pro-immigration group: politicians. Pandering towards immigrants through promises of non-sustainable, yet ever-growing social programs provides politicians a dependable, dependent base of voters. New York Democrats met Irish immigrants fresh off the boats, handed them a coin and told them to vote for Tammany Hall. President Obama has raised these stakes through taxpayer-subsidized health care.

The third group in favor of immigration is the liberals, bearing a guilt they can only exorcize by spreading our wealth (not just theirs) and assigning themselves as the official *bother's-keeper* of illegals. This concept also provides them a giddy sense of superiority, for beneficence always comes at a price. Liberals expect illegals to show continuing appreciation and bondage to their causes. This is empowering for any rulers. That is, until they discover what kings of yore always feared: alms for the poor actually creates resentment and unrest within the peasantry.

Liberals have been indoctrinated by elitist-controlled academes and elitist-controlled media to feel guilty for their lifestyles: their abundance, their diet, their entertainment, their health, their large homes, their formal educations and the evil of *conspicuous consumption*. It is also preached to this group that America is blessed only by sheer luck. And that we attained our high standard of living only through exploitation of all other peoples in the world. We should repent. Or so they say.

Atonement is at hand for this group by welcoming the less fortunate, by sharing *our* abundance, by allowing masses of immigrants to invade our nation and partake freely of that which we have, through generations, worked dearly to create. In essence, liberals are advising all of us to be party to the destruction of our own culture and country.

The fourth group, most dangerous and most clandestine, is the *elitists*. They manipulate the liberals to do their bidding. The elitists derive from the beyond-liberal, Über rich, or are descendants of long-standing, socially-elite families. They contribute money to politicians, thereby controlling our national agenda and national debate. They control our most prestigious universities, ensuring our country's so-called intelligentsia are of like-mindedness, aping the elitists' doctrine. Their money chooses our Senators and Presidents.

Always *sub rosa*, the motivations of the elitists are completely different from that of their minions: the liberals and politicians. Elitists' motivations are much darker.

They wish the original plan of America be subverted. For they have a greater plan.

Elitists believe in *one-world* government.

Their worst historical moment was the *Treaty of Westphalia* (1648). For here, in an area of northwest Germany, a treaty was signed to end thirty years of European religious wars (Catholics against Protestants). It established the borders of European nations and resulted in a movement that is vile to elitists. That movement is *nationalism*. Why is this term an epithet to elitists? Because they feel the world would be best served under one government; not a patchwork quilt of nations competing amongst themselves. Elitists believe that competition among nations is responsible for all the ills of the world.

But who would run a *one-world* government? As their favorite author H. G. Wells constantly preached, a core of all-knowing, altruistic, benevolent leaders. In other words, *Über* rich, Hobbesian elitists. (Their hated author is George Orwell. That is why our school children are no longer required to read *Animal Farm* and *1984*). Elitists believe that their money (used to accumulate power) provides them wisdom and vision sorely lacking within the rest of us.

The elitists know what is best for all. No messy democracy is required.

To help foster their goals, this group has a ready-made army. This army is comprised exclusively of immigrants. Enough of these masses washing back and forth across national borders translates to borders having no meaning. Cultural differences (meaning all cultures) would disappear under elitist reign. So would any sense of *nationalism*, for it is the true evil to elitists.

And if social programs can be flooded by indigent immigrants, thereby bankrupting nations, the goal of elitists is met even more rapidly.

Catastrophes await

We are quickly losing distinction as a nation. We do not control our own borders. We do not control our social program costs. To what end will this lead?

Four catastrophes:

First is a loss of our national identity. Self-reliance, independence, free-enterprise, wealth, abundance and freedom are destined for the trash bin as we march ever more quickly to the baton of elitists. We have already moved far in that direction during this new century. Over $20 **Trillion** in national debt speaks of a country unable to pay for ever-expanding social services and social programs. We have become a debtor nation. We are not able to service that debt unless we print more and more money. Worthless currency is how nations express bankruptcy.

Second is the end to the *path-of-more*. The system that allows us to create abundance, wealth, enlightenment, self-fulfillment, health, freedom and all the scientific marvels of the future is being strangled. Eventually it will die. Abundance creates surplus. And derived from surplus is the financing of today's dreams for tomorrow's realities.

Third is the physical loss of our nation. The American Southwest is rapidly being ceded to Mexico.

A nation that cannot colonize a land with a majority of its own people will never hold that land. That is why Mexico lost Texas, then California, Arizona, New Mexico, Nevada, Utah and parts of Wyoming and Colorado. They never controlled it to begin with.

According to the census of 2010, Hispanics were **37.6%** of the population of California, and growing. Texas has the **exact same number**. Arizona is at **20%** and so is Colorado. New Mexico is the largest number at a near-majority of **46%**. These numbers do not include illegal aliens afraid or unwilling to respond to a census for obvious reasons.

Assimilation of these numbers into American culture is impossible. And without assimilation Mexico will reconquer our Southwest.

Already the United States is beginning to unravel.

Europe is well into this process. Middle-Easterners and North-Africans are flooding into European cities. But there are groups beginning vocal opposition. Yet, with the numbers against them, the ability of Europe to save its indigenous people and their culture is doubtful.

Fourth is the capitulation of Independent and Conservative forces. The liberals, steered by elitists, are making sure their agenda for America's cultural dissolution marches forward. The most striking way they are accomplishing this is through the Census. In the 2010 Census, Democrats were successful in allowing a statistical analysis of population numbers to be substituted for the way the Census has been counted since we became a nation. This was justified in order to account for all lower class or homeless people that, supposedly, cannot be found and counted. However, this was merely cover for allowing illegal immigrants to be counted. This skewed number will change the electoral count of the States. Red (Republican) States will diminish in electoral votes while Blue (Democrat) States will increase.

And another Democrat President will ensure that a large portion, if not all, of the **12 Million** illegal aliens here become citizens. This, in turn, will assure that

Democrats gain both Houses of Congress. And then the Elitists can manipulate their liberal minions to increase the rate of America's cultural dismemberment.

Presidential voting has landed squarely on the side of immigration lovers. And they owe it all to the Obama Administration changing how we have conducted the census for over 250 years.

And it was done without a single shout of protest.

An unknown problem

How many spies have blended in among invading immigrants? How many terrorists? How many illegal drug shipments? We do not know because we have not attempted to find, arrest or deport the majority of these persons. We do not maintain a database on them. We will probably only find out when our latest military weapon designs appear in China or Russia or Iran only months after deployment here. Or when a nuclear bomb is detonated within one of our major cities.

For Americans to allow open borders and unchecked illegal immigration is insane. We are the Number One target of fanatics and terrorists across the globe. We should be capturing and jailing or deporting *every single person* illegally entering this nation or whose visa has expired.

Even if terrorists or spies enter our country legally, we do a poor job at following their movements. But, for illegal entries, we are virtually helpless. It would make more sense for a terrorist to impersonate another ethnicity, then clandestinely cross one of our borders and blend in among the mass of illegals. Terrorists know that America does not go after illegal aliens with any fervor. Why not impersonate one?

Through inaction on illegal immigration, we are putting America's safety at risk. We are at war. We should act like it.

Solutions

For the United States, we still have a thin window of time to reverse this trend. Solutions to this threatening problem do exist. However, as stated at the beginning of this article, they require a *hard* path. As adults, we should know that easy answers to intractable problems seldom exist. Now is the time for us to harden our resolve and take necessary steps. Below are listed what we must do. All are necessary for a successful outcome. All must occur now. Time is short:

End All Immigration

Yes, this means **all** immigration. We are in no need of a surplus work force. We have no empty land that requires settling.

America is full up. *Completa. Ocupado.*

No more war refugees from failed nations. God only knows how many terrorists are in this mix. We are potentially importing terrorism into the heart of our country. What are we thinking?

We need no more cheap labor. We are trying to raise wages, not suppress them. And, regardless of liberal arguments, raising minimum wages does not raise the overall standard of living. Like government jobs, it is an artificial manipulation of the market place that decreases the number of employed, moves many workers from full-time status to part-time (with loss of benefits) and forces business to raise prices of goods and services in order to cover increased costs (a contributor to inflation).

What about skilled labor the U.S. lacks? Would we still allow business to import these people on work visas? Absolutely not. We need to end this and revoke all work visas now. The so-called *American* corporations use a loop-hole in our immigration policy to allow wholesale importation of labor. They plead that the skilled workers they require our lacking in our own populace. This is a myth, sham, lie; choose a term.

Computer programmers and engineers from Asia and India flood into our country under this guise. Yet our own people with these skills go unemployed. Understanding the real reason hi-tech companies take advantage of this loop-hole is quite simple. They pay this imported labor pool half of what they would pay a U.S. worker with the same skillset. We are not talking about production-line jobs. These U.S., unemployed workers are degreed, university graduates. Yet they are somehow unqualified for American jobs. During every recession, we tell unemployed and future workers that the jobs lost are lost forever. The unemployed are told to go back to school and *retool* their skills to fit the future, hi-tech, high-paying jobs. Yet we are allowing those exact jobs to be sourced to immigrants, at a 50% discount. Do we still wonder why large corporations call themselves *International*, and not American? The only patriotism they abide is what our laws force upon them.

But what of the future Einstein, the physicist or mathematical *savant* that could allow the U.S. to leap-frog our international competitors? For such gifted people, allow Congress to vote them citizenship or permanent immigration status. However, the law should restrict this to no more than five persons a year (there really is not that many true savants out there that wish to immigrate to the U.S.). Such Congressional action should require a two-thirds vote of the Senate. Additionally, a high-profile political refugee from a totalitarian state could be included within this annual five person allotment.

Would we still allow Tourist visas or Business visas or Student visas? Certainly, but only for a very limited window; four weeks for tourist, six weeks for business and annual-term-of-school for students. A tourist could drive across America and back easily within this time frame. And in the case of a business visa, anything over six weeks is deemed employment, which is illegal. We do not want other nationalities taking American jobs.

But what if a job requires more than six weeks? As with other countries, the person would have to leave our country at the end of six weeks, stay out for six weeks, then reapply for another visa. If the corporation is willing to wait for such a person, then perhaps they really do possess a skill unavailable within the U.S. labor pool. As China requires, a business visa would need sponsorship of an American corporation. If the person actually has business here, a corporation should burden the responsibility of ensuring this person goes where they say they are going, stay for the approved time and leave on-time. Anything goes wrong and the corporation faces a large fine. If the business visitor is arrested for a crime, so the corporate person issuing the sponsor letter should be arrested and charged with aiding and abetting a criminal.

Tourist visas should be pre-approved before any person steps foot upon American soil. The application should be accompanied by a planned itinerary including hotel names. What if they do not know at which hotel they will stay? Don't come to the U.S. The day of foreigners backpacking across America is dead. Would we deprive them of the real American experience, freedom to roam wherever the winds take them? Yes, we would. That experience is reserved for U.S. citizens only. If a tourist deviates from their itinerary without notification, an arrest warrant is issued immediately. Once tracked down, they are arrested and deported. As Asians are wont to say, very sorry.

What if a visitor wishes to change their itinerary? No problem. They go to the nearest Federal immigration office and register the change.

What would be the restrictions on a Student visa? The student must travel directly to the city or town in which the school resides. Any desire to become a tourist during school breaks requires pre-applying for a tourist visa. If the foreign student is invited to go home with U.S. citizen "Buddy", then Buddy has to sign the visa application as a sponsor, same as a business does. Buddy also assumes the legal responsibility of a corporate sponsor.

A tourist, businessman, or student on a visa within our country must carry their stamped visa (i.e. passport) and approved itinerary at all times. This used to be a requirement in many other countries. European hotels were once required by their governments to keep a foreigner's passport until check-out.

Is this not a gross violation of a foreigner's freedom?

No, because foreigners within any country only have the freedoms as annunciated by the host country. Will not other countries apply the same measures to U.S. citizens visiting them? Some already do. For those that do not, if they are smart they will incorporate the

same measures. It's a byproduct of a dangerous time.
We are at war. We should expect inconveniences.

No Wall

Building a wall to deter immigration is folly. Unless we
are prepared to create a one-hundred-yard, mined, *no-man* zone with guards atop the wall, ready to kill
invading men, woman and children, there is little sense
to the idea. Additionally, even this extreme measure
can be circumvented via tunnels. Americans are not
ready to endorse such efforts, yet.

The only way to prevent the current illegal immigrant
assault is through denial of why these people come. It
is for jobs and access to our social services. When we
remove these incentives, the bulk of illegals will stop
coming here. The balance we arrest and deport.

Building a wall is not only folly, it is a waste of taxpayer
money that should be used for federal forces to arrest
illegals, and facilities within which to detain them.

This does not mean we abandon security along our
borders. Just the opposite. We need to increase our
U.S. border patrol and augment it with National Guard
troops, contributed and supported by each State. We
need to upgrade our security hardware with the latest
generations of non-lethal weapons (i.e. propelled nets,
Tasers, knock-out gases, rubber bullets) and
surveillance and detection tools (i.e. drones, infrared,
above-ground and below-ground sensors).

And if the above prescription fails, then we create the mined, no-man zone, with sensor probes buried a hundred feet down. It is still cheaper than a wall, more effective and removes the responsibility of pulling a trigger out of the hands of an American. A constant recording in appropriate languages, blasted through speakers would advise persons they are entering a minefield. Any injury or death is their fault, not America's.

No Amnesty

Congress passed the Immigration Control Act of 1986, which was signed by President Reagan. It was designed to provide a path to citizenship for an estimated 3.2 million illegal aliens. In this it succeeded. Obviously all other aspects to prevent further illegals failed. Since this time another estimated 11 to 12 million illegals now reside within the United States. In 30 years our illegal alien population grew 400%. Assuming this rate remained linear (which is unlikely), this translates to nearly 50 million additional aliens flocking across our borders by 2046. Just as lack of policing any law encourages increased crime, amnesty encourages new waves of illegal immigration. To even discuss amnesty or paths to citizenship is tantamount to declaring our borders open to all who wish to invade. No more discussion of amnesty.

Deport all illegal immigrants

Regardless of ethnicity, all illegal persons in our country must leave. Whether they have an expired visa or entered without one, they must depart. That is what our law states. And we are a nation of laws.

All illegals should be arrested and quarantined. Governments of their home countries should be notified in order to arrange their return. Failure of repatriation on the part of countries should have swift repercussions. All visas issued to citizens of their nations would be revoked and those persons within our country legally would also be deported. Enough angry calls home from their businessmen or tourists or students who are in our country will encourage them to collect their citizens.

Trade between our two countries would halt until the matter is solved. Any financial aid from the U.S. to countries involved would be suspended.

As to *anchor babies*, they can stay or go. However, the parents are leaving. The fate of the child is the parent's decision. If left behind, they become wards of the state. From this status they can be adopted by legal relatives, dispersed among foster parents or put up for general adoption. If the parents are truly loving-parents, they will take their babies with them. If a large number are left behind, this strongly indicates the original intent behind the births.

As to child refugees, they need to be humanely quarantined and their nationalities determined. Then they should be repatriated under the same methods as adults described above. With these actions America would be sending a strong message to the world. We will not abide illegal immigration into our country. And children will no longer be used as political pawns.

Repeal and replace the Fourteenth Amendment

Regardless the wishes of most of us, our Fourteenth Amendment to the Constitution states that a person born on American soil *is* a citizen. Using the historical background of the amendment, it could be argued that it was a Reconstruction amendment, a specific attempt to grant citizenship to former African-American slaves born here (which it was). But restricting any amendment or law to a narrow band of citizens rarely succeeds in Supreme Court arguments.

However, if we have the will, the amendment could be repealed and replaced in short order. One of our amendments was approved in a little over six months. Several others were approved within a year. If our Congress is unwilling to act, then the States should convene a Constitutional Convention. But make sure to note which Congressman and Senator is unwilling to support repeal. Then, get active and make sure they are not reelected.

The wording of the amendment is not complicated. It should state that *only* a person born to at least one parent of U.S. citizenship is a citizen. For the liberals that would affix their name to a birth certificate in order to circumvent our laws, there should be swift and strong punishment. The amendment should state that any proven fraud of parenthood would result in the child and the perpetrator being stripped of his or her citizenship. Naturally, deportation of all concerned would occur. A simple DNA test would resolve the issue of a child's origins.

Marriage of a non-citizen to a citizen would be similar and different than current rules. Yes, the non-citizen spouse would be allowed entry. However, the couple would have to remain married (versus divorce or annulment) for a period of five years. Then the spouse would be eligible to apply for citizenship. Background checks would be required. If positively vetted, the spouse would be subject to the same naturalization requirements as any applicant. If the spouse is negatively vetted, then entry will be denied, no matter valid marriage or not.

Additionally, the amendment should include a statement that persons illegally entering our country are combatants of a foreign assault and their legal status shall be that of prisoners-of-war. These rights are cited within Geneva Conventions that the United States has signed. State or federal judiciaries have no authority in this matter including, but not limited to, writ of *habeas corpus* or demands within a warrant. Illegal aliens are subject to military control and shall be held upon soil within U.S. military jurisdiction.

Perhaps Guantanamo may receive a second life. We could clean out our jails of illegal criminals and release them into Castro's care, returning the favor of the *Mariel* invasion.

Included should be wording as regards voting. Naturally, any non-citizen would be ineligible to vote no matter how long they have been here. Presentation of a non-reproducible, Federal ID (see next section) should be mandatory. The same quick scan and biometric check (see next section) should be applied. Anyone presenting a stolen or fraudulent ID should be arrested and jailed, then deported after serving their sentence.

The amendment should also state that neither Congress nor the President has the right to grant citizenship to any illegal alien. This would fall to Congress' annual allotment of five. The amendment should state that no President has the right of any blanket amnesty or immunity. No more war-torn refugees in our country. No more mass amnesties to illegal aliens.

War refugees should be assisted through Red Cross camps as has occurred for over a hundred years. Congress has the power to provide financial assistance. The UN (with American and, hopefully, our allies' participation) can help provide security for the camps. But do not put these camps on our soil. Do not give these people special treatment solely due to a status of being a citizen from a failed nation.

Can you imagine if we had allowed Palestinian refugees to migrate here from southern Lebanon? We would have imported the entire framework of Hezbollah into our nation.

If we are truly sympathetic to the Syrian refugees, the greatest gift we could provide is military training for every able-bodied adult, arm them with modern weapons and send them to fight for the freedom they wish us to give them freely. Under no circumstance should they be sent to the U.S. or Europe.

We did not start the Syrian war. Assad did. We are not a refuse bin for failed states.

Non-reproducible Social Security Card

Why not focus on driver licenses? There are three reasons. First, the States issue drivers licenses. If a liberal-influenced State, or one already infiltrated by illegal aliens, decided to ignore the law, it would cause a confrontation between state and federal. Second, States do not pool their licensing data within a central, national data base. Third, a Social Security card is issued by our federal government. Misuse, theft or counterfeiting of a card becomes a federal offense. Therefore, the federal government would have jurisdiction over non-responsive State governments in apprehending and prosecuting violators.

E-Verify, the federal system for verifying identity and status, is an employer check between form I-9 and employee identification provided. It incorporates most of the elements necessary for verifying citizenship or work-visa status. However, it has two fatal flaws. First, it is not mandatory. Second, identification documents incorporate no biometrics. Pictures and physical descriptions are not adequate precaution.

If a non-reproducible Social Security Card were required, along with making E-Verify mandatory, the system would have a chance of success. Such a system, using the centralized data base allowing employers to perform a quick verification of citizenship or visa status, would go a long way in identifying illegal aliens. It would also remove the major reason illegals come to this country: jobs.

A non-reproducible card should have an electronic chip imbedded along with a picture, description and biometric (i.e. thumb print). In a unit as small as a credit card reader a check of the central database could be performed in seconds. If a prospective employee is legal, the employer would be given an authorization code for the company's file. Even the smallest company could afford a card reader for a smart phone. It would be accompanied by a free, government app that could verify a biometric.

If an employer receives back from the electronic check that the biometrics do not match the file, that the card number does not exist or that the card is stolen or void, it becomes the responsibility of the employer to retain the card and immediately call the police in order that the potential employee be taken into custody and turned over to federal officers.

Real penalties for employers

The 1986 Amnesty Act included sanctions for any employer *knowingly* hiring illegal aliens. In order to escape prosecution, employers have used subcontractors to provide laborers. There currently is no law requiring end-employers to review the legal status of contract laborers working within their companies. If, by law, employers were required to verify legal status via a social security card and authorization number receipt, no matter how the labor was supplied, this would make end-employers responsible.

A fine of $10 thousand should be assessed for each illegal employee violation. Additionally, there should be a mandatory 1 year sentence for each violation (no suspended sentences). If one-hundred illegal aliens are found working at a company, a fine of $1 million would be assessed against the company *and* the legally-responsible person is going to jail for 100 years.

A CPA must sign a certified audit for a company's annual tax return. If he or she alters numbers fraudulently, he or she is looking at a prison term (along with whomever signed the returns on behalf of the company). This same method can be applied to employee verification. A person within management and responsible for verification must sign a federal document stating their responsibility and acknowledging the penalties involved.

Another area to be closed off is cash payments to laborers. Any company, no matter how small, should pay employees via company check. 99% of companies already comply. A payroll check is required to show deductions and is used in IRS investigations to track money. No one should be paid in cash. The same penalties as above should be applied.

Deny social services

No illegal alien should be allowed access to social services. If life-saving hospital services are requested it would be provided. However, citizenship status must be checked. If the person is illegal, they should be turned over to federal officers once they are well enough. Patients without a verified medical insurance card should be forced to present proof-of-citizenship (i.e. non-reproducible Social Security card). Those who do not will still be treated for life-threatening issues. Afterwards, police will detain these persons until legal status is determined. If they are found to be illegal, they will be turned over to federal officers and deported. If a hospital allows these persons to walk, then a major fine should be levied against the institution. If a hospital is financially hit hard enough, they will begin firing people responsible.

No children should be allowed into our school system without proof of citizenship or valid student visa. Illegals, along with their family members, should be arrested and deported. This would end the need and expense of bilingual education.

No welfare should be given to illegal families. If, prior to amending the Fourteenth Amendment, a child is considered a citizen yet the family is not, the child should be turned over to child services and the remaining family deported. Or the family can take the child with them. However, if the family takes the child, citizenship shall be stripped.

Punish repeat offenders

It is of no use to continually deport illegals if they know there is no penalty for trying again. If there is no consequence for breaking a law, how can we ever expect that law to be honored?

Every illegal arrested should be photographed, fingerprinted and DNA sampled (a quick swab of the mouth suffices). The information should be stored within a central data base prior to the person's deportation. (It would be interesting to see how many current crimes are solved via this data base). Males should be warned that the next incursion comes at a cost: detainment in a camp for six months. They should be shown videos of camp conditions and testimonies of those that were held prior.

With repeat offenders, women and children should be separated from males and deported. Males (sixteen and over) should be detained in camps for six months. Camps should be placed on U.S. military reservations, be under U.S. military jurisdiction and be subject to U.S. military oversight only. No state or federal judge would have authority here. No writs or warrants would be honored.

Camps should not be pleasant experiences. The food should be minimal and bland. Water should be the only drink. Any guard smuggling any contraband should be incarcerated in the same camp for one year. Armed U.S. soldiers should protect mined perimeters only, and not be required to police inmates within. No visitors are allowed except Red Cross inspectors as prescribed by Geneva conventions. The no-visitor rule would apply to reporters from the liberals' side. No freedom-of-the-press to whip up sentiments. No legal counsel is provided. No media or entertainment would be allowed. No sports equipment provided.

Inmates should be warned in their native languages that escape attempts will be met with capital punishment, meaning they will be shot by the guards, *if* they make it through the mine fields. Shooting is what is threatened of prison inmates. It is threatened of prisoners-of-war. After all, illegals are the troops of an invading army.

Pressure the countries involved

We have become a relief valve for overpopulated and failed countries. They send their overpopulation, their poor, their homeless, their huddled masses, their tempest-tost, their diseased, their illiterate and their criminals to our shores and across our borders. It is much easier than dealing with such problems within their nation.

What would happen if the relief valve did not work; if the U.S. refused entry and aggressively fought these incursions? What always happens when a relief valve does not work? Pressure builds and there is an explosion. That is what these failed nations are trying to avoid. They are divesting themselves of a growing problem by dumping it on America's doorstep. Therefore they are relieved of having to face problems of increasing population, increasing poor, increasing corruption, and increasing crime; results of bad economic and social policies.

If they will not stop their people from invading us, we must impose trade sanctions, end foreign aid, end financial aid, end military aid and stop propping up their currencies.

If illegals remained within their own countries, perhaps they would become the vanguard of change at home instead of an invading army zeroed in on our homeland. We are not helping the world by allowing these failed nations to avoid the results of their failed policies.

How to proceed

Ideas and writings are all well and good. But how are such changes to be implemented?

There are two paths. The first is at the Federal level. Every politician should be forced to state his or her position on immigration. If such words as *amnesty*, or *path-to-citizenship* are uttered, these politicians need to be driven from office and replaced with a person endorsing the ideas within this book.

Congressmen and Senators should be pressed to introduce legislation endorsing these ideas. Repeal and replacement of the Fourteenth Amendment is critical. However, Congress works slowly. This way it is allowed to avoid tough choices. It took Congress until 1875 to amend immigration law to ban prostitutes and convicts from entering our shores.

At the same time as pursuing Federal politicians, we need to attend to State legislators. Amendments can be introduced through a Constitutional Convention of the States.

And we should not leave out those candidates running for President. Only those vociferous in stopping illegal immigration by endorsing the ideas in this book should be supported. Candidates not supportive should be called upon publically to state their position on illegal immigration and to defend it via debate. They will lose the author's vote.

Our creed

We are Americans: We are the last, best hope of the world. Without the American example, the world will plunge into a thousand years of darkness.

We are Americans. We hold fast to the principles upon which this nation was founded. We believe in freedom of the individual. But that freedom comes with a price: self-reliance and personal responsibility. We do not rely upon others for our daily existence.

We are Americans. As with every other nation, we put the interests of *our citizens* before any others.

We are Americans. Although we have helped other nations time and again, we have no moral obligation to do so. We have no moral obligation to raise the rest of the world to our standard of living.

We are Americans. We will deter any manner of invasion or assault.

We are Americans. We are a charitable people, but disdain those who take advantage of our charity.

We are Americans. We respect our laws and expect visitors from other nations to respect them; just as would be expected of us if we were within their country.

We are Americans. We are a civil people, until the tensile of our tolerance is exceeded.

We say to all illegal aliens within our borders, please leave. You have exceeded our patience.

Author's Note:

Your comments are important and appreciated. Ratings and comments at the retailer's site for this book is very important to every author. Additionally, you may post a comment at:
author's facebook page:
https://www.facebook.com/mafarrellbooks
or at author's blog:
http://firethefederalgovernmentblog.com/